My Star
(All that I know)

Robert Browning
(1812–89)

OWAIN PARK
(b. 1993)

Andante tranquillo ♩ = 66

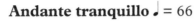

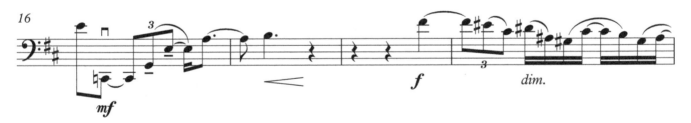

Duration: 3 mins

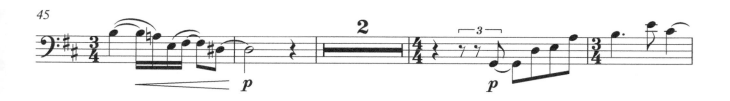

Agnus Dei II from *Missa brevis*

Canon Symphonizabis (*Canon in the unison*)

GIOVANNI PIERLUIGI da PALESTRINA (1525–94)
arr. BECKY McGLADE (b. 1974)

Duration: 2.5 mins

for the UNM Concert Choir's performance at the SWACDA Conference 2010, and for Joanna deKeyser, cellist

Heart, we will forget him!

Emily Dickinson
(1830–86)

BRADLEY ELLINGBOE
(b. 1958)

Duration: 3.5 mins

Lobet den Herrn, alle Heiden
BWV 230

Psalm 117

JOHANN SEBASTIAN BACH (1685–1750)
arr. BECKY McGLADE (b. 1974)

Duration: 7 mins

CELLO

CELLO

To a Skylark

Percy Bysshe Shelley
(1792–1822), adap.

KRISTINA ARAKELYAN
(b. 1994)

Duration: 3 mins

The Oak

Alfred, Lord Tennyson
(1809–92)

BECKY McGLADE
(b. 1974)

Duration: 3.5 mins

Recuerdo

Edna St. Vincent Millay
(1892–1950)

MARGARET BURK
(b. 1990)

Duration: 4 mins

CELLO

After Rain

Edward Thomas
(1878–1917)

HOWARD SKEMPTON
(b. 1947)

9

18

26

36

45

Duration: 3 mins

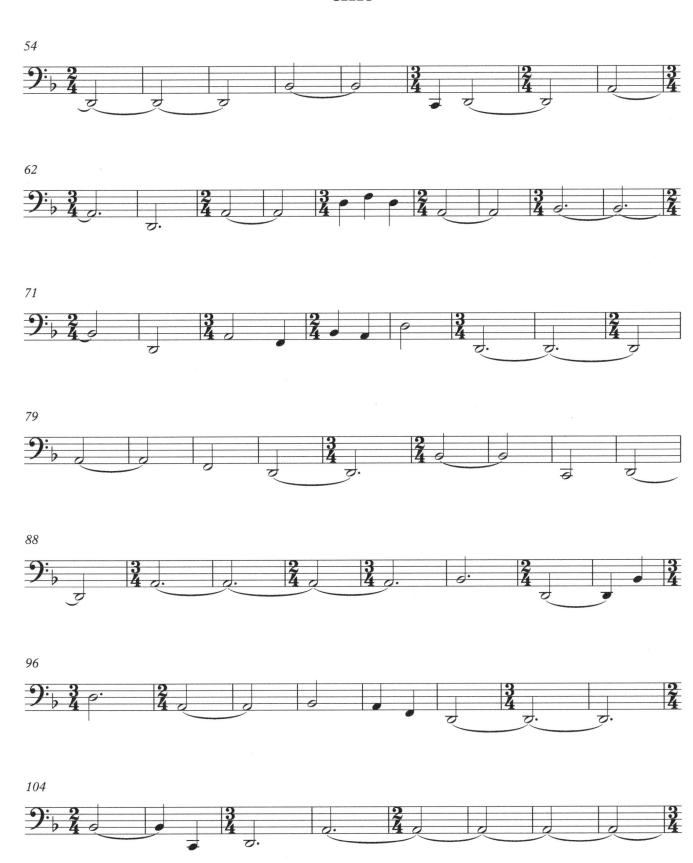

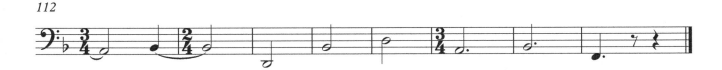

Vocalise
(Op. 34, No. 14)

SERGEI RACHMANINOFF (1873–1943)
arr. JONATHAN WIKELEY (b. 1979)

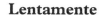

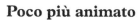

Duration: 4 mins

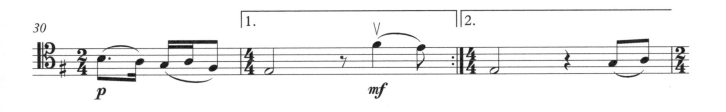

CELLO

Commissioned by the Avanti Chamber Singers, Artistic Director Rachel Rensink-Hoff,
for 'Ripple Effect', a collaborative project with cellist and sound engineer Kirk Starkey

Ripple Effect

Hildegard of Bingen (1098–1179)
Mother Teresa (1910–97)

SARAH QUARTEL
(b. 1982)

Duration: 5.5 mins

Come live with me

Words by Marlowe and
(attributed to) Raleigh

JOHN RUTTER
(b. 1945)

Duration: 3 mins

Music for Choir and Cello McGLADE

www.oup.com

ISBN 978-0-19-357029-0

9 780193 570290